Last Days of Spring

Miranda Maynard

This edition first published in paperback by
Michael Terence Publishing in 2023
www.mtp.agency

Copyright © 2023 Miranda Maynard

Miranda Maynard has asserted the right to be identified as
the author of this work in accordance with the
Copyright, Designs and Patents Act 1988

ISBN 9781800945074

No part of this publication may be reproduced, stored
in a retrieval system, or transmitted, in any form or
by any means, electronic, mechanical, photocopying,
recording or otherwise, without the prior
permission of the publisher

Cover image
Copyright © LightPoet
www.123rf.com

Cover design
Copyright © 2023 Michael Terence Publishing

Contents

Christmas Indulgence 1

1: Christmas at Aunt's (Christmas Invitation) 2

2: Grandfather Told a Christmas Story
   to his Grandchildren 7

3: The Grandchildren's Deep Sadness and Regret 11

4: Christmas Reflection 15

5: Special Christmas Memories 18

6: (Days After) A New Year at Grandfather's 21

7: Late Celebration 24

8: The Grandchildren's Deep Personal Reflection 29

9: Grandfather's Condition 32

10: The Visit 34

11: Last Time Together at Grandfather's 36

12: Last (Special) Sweet Memories 38

Footnote 39

Also by Miranda Maynard 41

Christmas Indulgence

At Christmastime Barry came over to his Aunt's house. In the dining room, the Family were having Christmas dinner. A roast.

In the sitting room. A front room. Barry was alone with Joe who popped in to give them a new bottle of wine. At the time of a seasonal feast.

"Aren't you going to eat?" said Joe.

"No. I have already eaten," replied Barry.

"I only stopped by to drop something off," gasped Joe.

"Nothing is new. There is always a Christmas fatty," laughed Barry.

1
Christmas at Aunt's
(Christmas Invitation)

At Christmastime, Perkins had been invited to his Aunt's house. On that day dinner guests were also invited, including family and their friends. A seasonal invitation.

Perkins joined his family for Christmas dinner. A roast. A provision had been made for vegetarians.

Perkins sat at the dining table with his family and their friends. The beautiful white tablecloth was set with fine silver cutlery, brass candlesticks, lit candles and napkins. Also included were paper hats and luxury Christmas crackers.

The invited dinner guests ate their hearty Christmas dinner.

Sitting at the dining table Perkins remained quiet while the dinner guests spoke. They conversed with each other.

From a dish Perkins' Aunt served food.

"How was work?" asked Aunt.

The startled secretary responded.

"Yeah. It's pretty busy. I am a typist. I just follow orders," replied Kirsty.

Perkins earlier listened to Kirsty a good conversationalist and listener. Perkins at a younger age desired Kirsty. The desirable secretary was attractive.

Perkins felt undesirable. A flabby gentleman with curiosity, he wondered about Kirsty. An interesting professional. Her secretarial skills were good.

Most guests feasted on turkey with trimmings and stuffing. The few others ate vegetarian food. This Christmas feast was an overindulgence. The overindulgent guests tucked into their Christmas dinner and dessert, a Christmas pudding. Followed by drinking a glassful of wine.

His Aunt paid attention to him.

"How was work?" asked Aunt.

Perkins worked for the Civil Service.

"It's bureaucracy as usual. It's all so… It's systemic," answered Perkins.

All the merry dinner guests seated at the dining table pulled a Christmas cracker. They each found a joke inside a cracker and a free gift. With enthusiasm, they read their joke enthusiastically.

Sitting and standing at the dining table every guest reached out and made a toast by celebrating. A seasonal celebration of Christmas.

Every guest was merry, jovial, jolly and exuberant. Usually at Christmas Perkins felt lonely. Normally living at home with his Mother. A single parent. Today at his Aunt's remained an exception. Perkins was in a happy mood. It was a Christmas treat. A candlelit Christmas dinner with Christmas dinner guests.

Perkins felt faint, tipsy and bloated after having eaten and drunk.

Eating her dinner Kirsty had a lack of appetite. Of course, Kirsty felt diet-conscious about her figure.

With disinterest, Kirsty had enough of being in the company of all the dinner guests sitting at the dining table. Getting up Kirsty asked to be excused first. This guest was the first one to get up and leave the dining table. Kirsty departed. A punctual departure. Kirsty was going away on a Christmas break with her friends tomorrow.

Perkins knew Kirsty already as a family friend. He was already acquainted. Earlier in the daytime, Perkins had renewed his acquaintanceship with Kirsty who had been reserved. Whilst everybody else talked away. (A few of them were unspiritual, worldly and materialistic.)

Perkins came into the luxurious lounge where he sat down in an armchair. There he joined the company of his nephew. Both of them sat nearby in front of the fire. In the dark, there was a glow of the fire and flickering light. They both kept warmed up from the warmth of room temperature.

"How is Christmas?" asked Nephew.

Perkins suffered from indigestion. He had mixed feelings about Christmas.

"I am stuffed. I mean this Christmas is full of gluttony. Such a thing overindulgence, isn't it? Everything is extravagant. All this extravagance," moaned Perkins.

"Really. Shouldn't Christmas be a time for festivity? To have fun?"

Perkins expressed his opinion and sentiment about Christmas.

"Quite. It's a time to get together and be festive and merry."

"Is Christmas that?" questioned Nephew.

Perkins differentiated between the opposite of Christmas.

"On the contrary. Christmas can be the complete opposite. A misery!"

The dreamy Nephew daydreaming (by the fire) expressed his sentimentality.

"I love Christmas," said Nephew dreamily.

"Did you get anything nice for Christmas?" asked Perkins.

"Oh! Yes. Toys," replied Nephew.

Perkins thought of the deep spirituality of Christmas as well as its true significance.

"I do lose interest in Christmas now. I reckon I have outlived it. A man my age. For me, it isn't Christmas anymore. The true essence of Christmas is lost. Shouldn't it be a spiritual thing?" said Perkins philosophically.

"Christmas is fun. I like to play," smiled Nephew.

"I am sure you do."

At present Perkins spent time with his playful Nephew. A good boy. Without the presence of the others. Perkins and his nephew stayed together till it was bedtime. For his nephew to go to bed. Perkins and his nephew went straight upstairs. Passing by along the way everybody else there downstairs. A few members of his family stayed behind. Going upstairs Perkins went to a bedroom where he joined his nephew's Mother in there. His Mother tucked him into bed. The Mother kissed her son on his forehead. A goodnight kiss. The Mother left her son and immediately came out of the bedroom. Perkins was left alone with his sleepy nephew.

Perkins decided to read a bedtime story to his nephew. The story was enchanting. It was filled with adventure and enchantment. The tale itself was magical, mystical and whimsical. His Nephew fell fast asleep on that late Christmas night. The sleeping nephew dreamt. His sweet dream was a paradise!

2
Grandfather Told a Christmas Story to his Grandchildren

In a big Victorian House, the Grandchildren played together. Entering the rooms of the house they played. The children had such fun. The Grandchildren were filled with curiosity going into different rooms. Some large rooms were spacious and other rooms were small. It had the distinctive smell of rich leather and polished and varnished wood, disinfectant, potpourri and room aroma.

Going out of a room, the Grandsons went upstairs. There was a flight of stairs. A winding staircase.

The daydreaming and lackadaisical Granddaughters lagged behind. They both entered an upstairs bedroom. There the curious Granddaughters went towards a beautiful intricate carved wooden wardrobe on the other side of the master bedroom. There both virgin Granddaughters stood admiring themselves in the mirror in virginal narcissism. They took narcissism from their reflection. Their beautiful mirror image. With joyful narcissism both Granddaughters were narcissistic. They both took narcissism of themselves at what they saw in the mirror of the wardrobe. The narcissistic reflection of themselves. Both vain Granddaughters had self-love for themselves.

Both Granddaughters hurried out of the double bedroom. Quickly they both joined up with the Grandsons who were waiting for them at the top of the landing. Overexcited from Christmas. Together they all went into a master bedroom where their beloved Grandfather and Perkins waited for them. At that time expecting them to come.

"We have been waiting," said Grandfather merrily.

All of the excitable Grandchildren were really happy at being in the presence of their peaceable Grandfather. They were joyful, excited, playful and delirious.

Grandfather was calm and merry as he sat down on a rocking chair. The obedient Grandchildren gathered around and listened to their Grandfather tell them a story. At present Perkins stood and stayed in the background. Perkins paid attention, listening to Arnold telling a story. It was truly a wonderful story!

By Grandfather's feet on the Persian carpet was a pile of wrapped-up Christmas presents. Grandfather gave the Grandchildren their gifts. The unsurprised Grandchildren expected this surprise. The excited Grandchildren ripped open the wrapping of their Christmas presents and their belated Christmas cards too.

Later that daytime. In the dining room, Perkins joined Grandfather and the Grandchildren for

Christmas dinner. Sitting with them at the dining table. This seasonal occasion was rather quite special.

Perkins got more Christmas joy at being with the Grandchildren than anything else. Nothing else would compare to this whatsoever. How his emotion was passionate!

He felt such a seasonal bliss at Christmastime. Perkins wanted to spend more time with them. He wanted to see them more often. Due to circumstances, it just wasn't possible. (Perkins had a commitment which he had to comply with.)

Afterwards, Perkins played with the playful Grandchildren. They all played hide and seek. All of the children hid while Perkins looked for them in their hiding places. Eventually, Perkins found only just two of them hiding. The others had somehow sneaked back. Perkins gave up on playing hide and seek. He lost interest in this game.

They rounded off Christmas Night together by sitting in front of the fire. The crackling fire. Together they all talked.

Grandfather was full of wisdom talking to the Grandchildren and those listening. With attentiveness, they all listened to their mellow Grandfather. Their Grandfather had such personal charm and humour too. Grandfather's mellowness and light-heartedness were traits of his.

Perkins stayed the night at Arnold's. The Grandchildren too also stayed over that night at Grandfather's house.

3
The Grandchildren's Deep Sadness and Regret

One night the Grandchildren and Perkins stayed up late that night. Charlotte and Amy and Barry and Nicholas were all deeply concerned for their Grandfather's health. Grandfather had retired. He had gone to bed.

Worrying, Charlotte expressed her concern.

"I do worry about Grandfather. He's not well. We are losing him," said Amy concernedly.

Charlotte spoke about her concern for her Grandfather.

"We are seeing less and less of our Grandfather. Aren't we? I hope Grandfather is alright."

"It just isn't the same without our Grandfather being here with us," gestured Barry.

Perkins tried to console the concerned and worried Grandchildren. They all fretted. All of the Grandchildren were feeling quite unhappy and miserable. All of them showed deep concern for their beloved Grandfather. They all felt quite distressed. They all had such deep love, affection, and concern and showed care for their Grandfather.

Doing nothing now, they all decided to play a game. They came into a room. The house light shone brightly. They all played Charades. Amy was good at this game. This stylish Granddaughter had such style.

The others showed enthusiasm for this game. Perkins showed some interest in Charades.

Charlotte, Perkins, Barry and Nicholas looked at Amy who stood in front of them at the front of the room. Amy was making graceful gestures and signs to express herself through action and thus made expressive signs. Amy kept cool as she expressed herself beautifully.

All at once they called out. They all tried to make a guess. All of them made a wrong guess. Eventually, Charlotte got it right. Charlotte's guess was correct!

After a considerable time, they all decided to end playing Charades. They all soon lost interest in playing this old-fashioned game. Their unenthusiasm and uninterest were apparent in playing this game. With unenthusiasm and half-heartedly they discontinued playing it.

During their last hour together all of the Grandchildren and Perkins talked about Grandfather during the course of that late night by the fire.

"We are losing our Grandfather. He's not well," repeated Amy.

"It's just not the same without Grandfather being here with us," mumbled Barry.

"Let's not worry. Grandfather will be alright. You'll see. He'll be just fine," reassured Perkins.

All of the Grandchildren who showed deep concern for Grandfather were somewhat consoled by Perkins' reassurance.

With deep feeling, Amy showed her appreciation. Amy had thoughtfulness for her Grandfather.

"We all have had a good Christmas with Grandfather. Shouldn't we be taking care of our Grandfather? Why don't you and I stay? We will take care of our Grandfather. You three go home," demanded Amy.

So Perkins and the Grandsons obeyed them. Charlotte confirmed to them that she intended to stay to take care of her Grandfather.

Subsequently, Perkins and the Grandsons went home. Charlotte and Amy stayed at Grandfather's house. Grandfather took joy and comfort as his Granddaughters stayed with him. Both Granddaughters attended to their Grandfather. Both Charlotte and Amy were attentive to their Grandfather. Simultaneously they both took care of their Grandfather. They also looked after their old Grandfather. They both took it in turns to cook for their Grandfather. Charlotte was good at cooking.

Charlotte and Amy did the chores and errands respectively, including all of the housework too.

Grandfather was becoming less house-proud as he was an old Gentleman. Suffering from bad health.

Grandfather remained unconcerned about his priorities at present.

Grandfather felt deeply loved by his caring Granddaughters. He appreciated how his caring and loving Granddaughters took care of him. The way both his Granddaughters cared for him remained truly a special bond of love for his Granddaughters.

With such appreciative love and affection, Grandfather remained thoughtful of his beloved Granddaughters. At this present time, Grandfather favoured them much more than his neglectful Grandsons!

4
Christmas Reflection

All of the Grandchildren and also Perkins saw Grandfather at his cosy cottage. At daytime in broad daylight. At that time Grandfather was holding a walking stick as he walked unsteadily. Grandfather apologised for how unwell he felt.

The concerned Grandchildren and Perkins sympathised. They had deep sympathy for Arnold. A bearded old Gentleman.

Grandfather lost his patience. Grandfather made an apology for being unsociable and neglectful to them. Grandfather waved his walking stick in the air. He was shaking.

"I do apologise. I am shaky. I am not well. I am going to lie down. I hope you don't mind. I can't see you right now. Not in this state. I don't mean to be rude. I hope you understand," apologised Grandfather.

All of the Grandchildren and Perkins stayed in the lounge which was finely furnished. They all sat down together and kept themselves warmed up by a fireplace. The fire was glowing in the dark. They felt the heat from the warmth of the fire. The room temperature rose. Sitting together they enjoyed their comfort. They took pleasure from being comfortable. Indulging by the fire. Keeping warm. Taking pleasurable comfort from the heat of the fire. The nice luxury of it.

Both Granddaughters felt dreamily romantic, lethargic and lackadaisical. Amy and Charlotte both romanticised having a dreamy romance. They took delight in the ambience. Amy was a romanticist and Charlotte a dreamer. They both reflected on Christmas. Looking back at Christmas. Their Christmas reflection was a joy and sweet memory.

"I liked it when I opened my presents. The present which Grandfather gave me. How can I forget it? He is such a lovely man," said Barry happily.

With girlish sweetness Charlotte was affectionate.

"Yeah. Me too. I got a dolly. Hey! A nice one. I love my Grandfather. Oh! How lovely of Grandfather," said Charlotte childishly.

"I got accessories to my train set. It's cool. I love it," said Nicholas appreciatively.

"Grandfather did not know what to give me. So, he gave me some money instead," said Perkins cheerfully.

With childish affection, Amy was emotional.

"Bless him! My Grandfather gave me a lovely watch. A lady's watch. Oh! How nice. Oh, how sweet of my Grandfather. I shall wear it with pride. I shall treasure it from the bottom of my heart," said Amy affectionately.

Suddenly a door opened Grandfather came out of a downstairs bedroom dressed up as Father Christmas. Taking out gifts from a Christmas stocking. He gave every Grandson and Granddaughter a Christmas gift. An additional Christmas present.

All of the Grandchildren's faces lit up with great joy. They were beatific from Father Christmas' surprising treat at Christmas. It remained an unexpected surprise! Both Granddaughters were completely surprised. Their charmed smiles were radiant. Feeling deeply emotional and blissful. The Grandsons too were well-pleased by their surprise. It was a pleasurable delight!

At once Grandfather masquerading as Father Christmas left all of the deliriously joyful Grandchildren and Perkins who felt cheerful and jolly.

Making a (seasonal) wish Grandfather went back to his bedroom.

5
Special Christmas Memories

Grandfather expected his Grandchildren and Perkins too to come round to his house today. At the time of them coming. Grandfather minutes earlier had waited for them.

Grandfather opened the front door and let them all in. Welcoming and greeting them. They also welcomed and greeted Grandfather. Appreciating his hospitality.

Entering, both Granddaughters kissed their Grandfather on the cheek with affectionate love.

Grandfather shook while standing still. He felt faint.

"I am terribly sorry. I am not well. I must lie down," apologised Grandfather.

They thought Grandfather was ill or he was simply a hypochondriac. Grandfather's hypochondria affected his state.

Grandfather wasn't eagerly keen on joining them. He did not join them, instead, he went back to his bedroom.

They all had grave concerns for their Grandfather. It gave them cause for concern. All of the Grandchildren as well as Perkins felt perturbed and agitated.

They all went into the warm lounge. They stayed there without Grandfather being present with them. It ended up being disappointing. They all became disappointed at Grandfather not joining them in conversation.

They all kept warm up by the fire. They felt ill at ease. Sitting together they all reflected on their Christmas. They all had a good and bad Christmas. One of them was indifferent to their families coming and staying. Everything depended on the circumstances.

"It's a shame Grandfather is not with us. Again, he is ill. What is wrong with him?" said Barry worriedly.

Realising they were depressed. Amy the eldest Granddaughter agitated them. Amy objected to any of them being depressed. Barry was a depressive.

"C'mon. Let's not worry. Let's be merry. Let's have a good Xmas," said Amy positively.

Charlotte blew her nose with a tissue.

"I quite agree. Let's not be miserable. Aren't there enough miseries in the world," murmured Charlotte.

"It makes a change being here at Grandfather's. Why on earth do I have to put up with my parents quarrelling? Now what was the best thing about your Christmas?" asked Nicholas.

"Actually, coming to my Grandfather's. Staying with him. That's the highlight for me. My Xmas!" smiled Amy.

"For me, opening a present which Grandfather gave me," exclaimed Barry admittedly.

"Yeah. Just being with Arnold. For sure. That was the best thing for me. It made such a difference staying at my Grandfather's," grinned Perkins.

At present they were unaware of their Grandfather standing behind them by an ajar door while eavesdropping. As they were all too engaged in a conversation, they had unawareness of it. They had unnoticed their Grandfather standing behind a door. To any of them. To any of them talking or joining in a conversation, it just did not occur to them. An unnoticed inattentiveness from them.

6

(Days After)
A New Year at Grandfather's

A few days after New Year's Day Perkins and all of the Grandchildren came to see their old Grandfather at his house. Both the Granddaughters cooked. They both treated their Grandfather with good intentions.

In the dining room sitting at the dining table together, they ate a nice dinner and had a drink. The Grandsons, Perkins and Grandfather ate a roast dinner and the strict diet-conscious Granddaughters had a vegetarian meal. Amy was an Epicure as well as a vegan.

Grandfather shook. Feeling unwell Grandfather retired. Going to his bedroom to lie down and rest.

Afterwards, Perkins, the Grandsons and Granddaughters helped with the chores in the kitchen. Charlotte washed up and Amy dried up the dishes with a dry, clean tea towel. Nicholas and Barry cleaned up the kitchen. Nicholas swept the kitchen floor and Barry cleaned up and wiped the surface of the tabletop with a clean cloth. Perkins used a dustpan and brush to pick it up off a clean floor.

Staying together in the lounge warming up from a fire. They all had a good conversation. They each told their New Year resolution, which everyone blurted out and shared amongst themselves. Henceforth they each expressed themselves. Those listening seemed satisfied at them mentioning their New Year resolution. Their reticence was evident.

Suddenly the topic changed to everyone's relief.

"How was your Christmas? New Year?" asked Amy.

"So and so. My Christmas was lonely. Alone with my Mother. Things changed when I stayed at my Grandfather's at Christmas. My Christmas just transformed. I just can't explain it. It was great just being with my Grandfather. And meeting you all too. You lot. I had a ball. In a sort of really strange way this Christmas was special!" expressed Perkins.

Amy smiled. A girlish smile. "My New Year was jolly good," paused Amy. "How about yours?"

"It wasn't bad at all. It could have been better," said Barry negatively.

Charlotte showed optimism.

"It's a start of a New Year. Isn't it time to be optimistic at the New Year?" said Charlotte optimistically.

"I admit I do have aspirations. I do lack ambition. I ought to be ambitious," said Nicholas unashamedly.

In the lounge. Sitting by a fire they all kept themselves warmed up. Warming up from the heat of the fire. In a dim room both Granddaughters felt rather excitedly romantic at being in a glow of a fire. Their glowing presence was an electrifying enchantment.

Perkins and the Grandsons engaged in a conversation. Perkins was a good conversationalist. A mathematician talking about his obsessive mathematical obsessions – and theories. Perkins's theoretical analytic explanations and analysis. A theorist and mathematician analyst.

7
Late Celebration

In the study, Grandfather sat on a comfortable swivel chair at his desk. In the study, there were books, paperbacks and hardcovers. All of the set of encyclopaedias were in a glass cabinet and many books were on bookshelves.

Grandfather was a Bibliophile. (His bibliophilism began when he became a professional Librarian as he engaged in Librarianship which he pursued.)

Once he used to be a Librarian. Formerly this former Librarian had bibliophilistic possession obsessions.

At this present time, Grandfather invited his Grandchildren and Perkins individually to come into his study. One by one. Grandfather cautioned every one of them. With some sort of parental love, he cautioned them.

Perkins was the first one to enter the study. Grandfather tolerated Perkins. Grandfather was tolerant of Perkins. At this time Grandfather cautioned Perkins for being undisciplined.

"My dear boy! You're mathematical. You work in the Accounts Department. Do be ambitious. Do aim high. Don't be mediocre. Not this mediocrity. Why don't you write a Maths textbook? Do something. Don't be mundane. Be competitive. That's all I have to say on this matter. You can go. Tell Barry to come in next," said Grandfather calmly.

Perkins listened to Grandfather advising him. He had enough of the advice being offered.

Perkins came out of the study. He passed by Barry along the way. Then Barry came into the study next. Barry came up to the desk. Then he listened to what his Grandfather had to say.

"Stop this malarkey. Get on with your work. Stop chasing girls and concentrate on your work. That's the best thing to do. Remember they are self-made. You are not!" cautioned Grandfather.

Standing opposite Grandfather seated. Barry felt rather humiliated, sullen and embarrassed.

"Yes, Grandfather," murmured Barry.

At once Barry came out of the study in utter embarrassment. There he found Nicholas waiting outside the study. By the door.

"Go in! You're next," urged Barry.

Going into the study. Nicholas listened to his Grandfather's advice.

"Nicholas. Just a word. You're doing far too much. Slow down! Try to concentrate on one thing at a time. Don't panic. Don't worry. You worry too much. Get used to doing things," advised Grandfather.

Nicholas cooled down as he quickly left the study. Unappreciative of his Grandfather's advice.

Simultaneously both Charlotte and Amy came into the study. Standing together by the desk, with an eager interest they both paid attention to their Grandfather. Grandfather sitting on a swivel chair stirred. He moved position. Grandfather spoke to Amy first before Charlotte.

"There's not much to say. Amy, you are versatile. My talented Granddaughter. You're motherly. Do take care of everyone. Do look after them. I insist. I am proud of you. You are special. You're blessed. You're a blessing. You're my favourite Granddaughter!" said Grandfather proudly.

Did Charlotte disapprove of Grandfather's favouritism for Amy? Charlotte resented it! Charlotte may have been jealous of Amy naturally.

Grandfather got up. He struggled to get up. Grandfather felt stiff. He moved towards Charlotte. His Granddaughter. Grandfather put his arms around Charlotte. With love, he tried to comfort his Granddaughter.

"Last but not least. Charlotte, you're passionate. Do listen. Don't disobey. Do as you are told. Child, keep your faith. Don't ever lose it," advised Grandfather.

Both emotional Granddaughters listened to their Grandfather. They both re-joined the others who were waiting for them to come out.

Last Days of Spring

All of the Grandchildren (apart from Perkins) as it appeared, unappreciated their Grandfather's advice, Grandfather's wisdom! Most of them either obeyed or disobeyed their Grandfather. One of the Grandsons remained stubborn. Their mellow Grandfather possessed wisdom!

Perkins joined up with the Grandchildren. Charlotte, Amy, Barry and Nicholas. They all went into the dining room. There they found an oriental ornate vase and beautiful ornaments as well as a tray with tumblers full of blackcurrant juice on top of a dining table and an antique somewhere placed in a corner of the dining room. None of them had seen this lovely antique ever before. Was this furniture second-hand? In good condition.

"Now. Tell me. What do you think of what Grandfather said?" said Amy curiously.

Perkins responded in an honest way.

"Grandfather said a lot of good things. He does wish us well."

"Yeah. He did. Didn't he," mumbled Nicholas.

"We must listen to our Grandfather, shouldn't we? He has wisdom," said Charlotte insistingly.

"I agree. We must listen," smiled Amy.

"Shouldn't we listen to our Grandfather?" said Charlotte repeatedly.

"Quite. We must," stuttered Perkins.

Wearing his slippers Grandfather came into the dining room. Grandfather picked up a tray off the dining table. Everybody helped themselves to a tumbler. Grandfather put the tray back down on the dining table.

"Let's toast!" insisted Grandfather.

They all stood together and raised their tumblers. They all made a toast. All of them celebrated the New Year with merrymaking as well as amusement. The actual late celebration of it had amused them all.

8
The Grandchildren's Deep Personal Reflection

Grandfather stayed away. He spent time away at his second home.

At a home, the Grandchildren stayed together. They all reflected on their beloved Grandfather. How Grandfather went away and stayed away.

All of the Grandchildren had stuck around until Perkins had come. As Perkins came, they all together talked about Grandfather. They had a deep reflection on their Grandfather.

"Is Grandfather better?" asked Perkins.

"Grandfather has not been well," answered Amy.

Charlotte mentioned her Grandfather's condition.

"Grandfather is senile. He stays in bed. Grandfather has been unwell," confirmed Charlotte.

"Oh! What a pity!" they said.

Perkins thought of his Christmas.

"My Christmas was a bore and misery until I came to Grandfather's. Things just drastically changed for the better. I had a fabulous time at Grandfather's. We all did. Didn't we?"

"By magic. We had a lovely time," smiled Amy.

"We got some nice presents," mentioned Barry.

"Yeah. We did. Wasn't it wonderful? Grandfather was Father Christmas! Truly that's the most wonderful thing about it," grinned Nicholas.

Amy had cause for concern for her Grandfather.

"I worry about my Grandfather. His health. I do fear the worse," said Amy concernedly.

"We all do. Don't we?" mumbled Barry.

"We are losing our Grandfather. Aren't we?" said Charlotte sadly.

"Just remember one thing. Grandfather has such love for us. We do have such love for our Grandfather. Let's remember that. Our wonderful times with Grandfather," reminded Amy consolingly.

"Yes. Let us," smiled Charlotte.

They all found solace in being together again. At this time of the New Year. The Grandchildren preferred to be alone together without their Grandfather being present with them. (Grandfather had been grumpy the last time they all saw their Grandfather.)

At Christmas and after the New Year. All of them being together alone with Grandfather made such a difference. A seasonal ecstasy and joy. Sitting together they remembered what their Grandfather recalled. His special fond memories. The garden picnic with his beloved wife and Grandfather bowling at the green at a bowling club and last but not least the luxury of a new Persian carpet which Grandfather gratified by taking comfort in. He took pleasurable relaxation satisfaction from it. He unwound in a relaxed fashion.

9
Grandfather's Condition

At home all alone together, Perkins and the Grandchildren reflected on their beloved Grandfather. They had a sense of fatalism. They knew their Grandfather would die. His general health was bad. Grandfather's health deteriorated. They fretted. What could they all do for their Grandfather? The Granddaughters took the initiative to do something, to look after and care for their Grandfather. They felt hopeless as Grandfather rejected Perkins and his Grandsons. Attending to their Grandfather was their main priority!

With attentiveness, both Granddaughters attended to their Grandfather. Giving their Grandfather the care, love and attention needed. Grandfather required their help and support.

With both Grandsons absent. Both Granddaughters took care of their Grandfather They both looked after their Grandfather. Knowing sooner or later their beloved Grandfather would die!

They took their time to attend to their Grandfather. Both loving Granddaughters were attentive to their Grandfather. Both caring Granddaughters did their best to take care of their Grandfather and to look after him. In his old age, Grandfather became senile in his condition. He expected too much from them. Grandfather demanded too much from his overworked Granddaughters having such obsequiousness. Their submissiveness of an obedient nature. They both remained obsequious to their attention-seeking and hypochondriac Grandfather. Both Granddaughters were loving, caring and attentive to their sick Grandfather with bad health. Grandfather stayed in bed and remained bedridden for days and nights.

10
The Visit

The Grandchildren and Perkins came to visit their Grandfather. Today they came to see their Grandfather at his house. Arriving there they had already found a visitor, a Priest alone with Grandfather. At that time Grandfather was taking his last rites!

Perkins and the Grandchildren made a brief visit. With intentional obligation. They all visited their Grandfather who remained bedridden. With deep concern for their Grandfather. They felt so sad! Staying with their dying Grandfather.

That night Grandfather passed away.

Perkins and the Grandchildren attended their Grandfather's funeral.

Both Granddaughters in mourning dressed in black and wore gloves and veils.

The sad mourners, friends and families were deeply mournful and bereaved. Standing together they were feeling deep sorrow. This funeral itself was mostly a family affair. This funeral today was a sad day!

***

At home together again. Suffering from bereavement. During their time of mourning for Grandfather, they kept away. They avoided and eluded everybody on purpose. A purposeful intent. They also isolated themselves. Together amongst themselves, they mourned for their Grandfather. They stayed together and grieved for their Grandfather. They all remained housebound. All of them felt mournful, bereaved and in deep sorrow! As they felt too much grief and sadness. How could any of them really cope and live without their Grandfather? Of course, naturally, their life for them would never ever be the same again!

11
Last Time Together at Grandfather's

Going to Grandfather's house for the last time. A loved one and deceased.

They all entered the lounge. There the Grandchildren and Perkins saw a big silver-framed photograph of their Grandfather with his wife Henrietta. A marriage of bliss! It was noticeably conspicuous.

Deeply missing their Grandfather. They all felt too mournful, bereaved and sad. All of them felt deep bereavement. They all had deep memories of their Grandfather. A loved one!

One of the Granddaughters cried. They gave comfort to each other. They each consoled Amy first then followed by everybody else.

"Grandfather gone! He's taken away from us," said Amy mournfully.

Perkins feeling deep emotion had expressed his affection.

"Let's remember Grandfather the way we should," said Perkins sadly.

"We all miss our Grandfather. Don't we? We all loved him," said Nicholas sorrowfully.

Perkins and the Grandchildren deeply missed their Grandfather. They all grieved for their Grandfather. Their loved one!

In remembrance, they all felt deep sorrow for their Grandfather. A bereavement!

Their deepest memories made them deeply saddened. They all cherished their deep memories of their Grandfather. They all deeply mourned the Grandfather!

How they all deeply loved their Grandfather. A sad loss!

12
Last (Special) Sweet Memories

The Grandchildren stayed away from everybody else including the rest of their families respectively.

At home together all of the Grandchildren reflected on their Grandfather. They shared their deep memories. Actually, they all felt a deep love for their late Grandfather. Since their beloved Grandfather passed away, life for them would never be the same again!

They all felt such deep sorrow. Both passionate Granddaughters cried.

The Grandsons and their relatives grieved for their Grandfather. In their time of grief, they comforted and consoled one another. Sharing the very same things in common which were deep sorrow and bereavement. All of them felt deeply mournful, sad and bereaved.

Footnote

Perkins' and the Grandchildren's final last months with their beloved Grandfather probably remained the best days of their lives. For personal sentimental reasons. None of them could really express their emotion and explain it. Neither of them could describe the emotions and personal sentimentality that they all felt for the late Grandfather.

Their past remained a memory. Naturally, it was something which was poignant, evocative and evocable that came to their minds.

- THE END -

Also by Miranda Maynard

*Available worldwide from Amazon
and all good bookstores*

www.mtp.agency

www.facebook.com/mtp.agency

@mtp_agency

www.ingramcontent.com/pod-product-compliance
Lightning Source LLC
LaVergne TN
LVHW051217070526
838200LV00063B/4948